THE BEST HEROES

Written by
Doug Kauffmann

Illustrated by
Cherry Smith

The Best Heroes

Written by Doug Kauffmann
Illustrated by Cherry Smith

ISBN:
978-1-940645-88-9 (softcover)
978-1-940645-89-6 (hardcover)

Courier Publishing
Greenville, South Carolina

Printed in the United States of America

The author wishes to thank Cherry Smith for her illustrations and Butch Blume and the staff of Courier Publishing for their assistance in bringing this book to life.

COURIER PUBLISHING

This book is dedicated to all who are champions on behalf of children, starting with their own children.

It is also dedicated to the doctors, nurses, caregivers and staff in medical facilities who have been our "Best Heroes" and have sacrificed so much in caring for those patients and families who have battled the COVID-19 pandemic.

"The godly people in the land are my true heroes! I take pleasure in them!"
— *Psalm 16:3, NEW LIVING TRANSLATION*

It was the day of the big championship game. My heroes, the New York Giants, were playing the Green Bay Packers, a team I had never heard of before. I had no idea where Green Bay was or what a Packer was, but I knew this: They were the bad guys.

On the way to the game, a man in the subway saw me carrying my Giants pennant. "Who do you think is going to win the game today?" he asked. I answered politely, "The Giants," but I thought to myself: What's wrong with him? How can he not know the Giants can't lose? Heroes don't lose!

My dad took me into New York City that day. I had never been so excited as I was a few days earlier when Dad came home from work and asked me if I would like to see the Giants play for the championship. He knew I loved the Giants. I bragged about them all the time. "Sure!" I said. "But can we get tickets?"

"Oh yes," Dad said. "I've already got them!"

That was the nicest thing anybody had ever done for me. My dad took the time to think about what his little kid wanted most in the world—and I didn't even have to ask! I was the youngest of four children, but I really felt chosen that night.

The day of
the game was
bitter cold, and
the wind was
whipping around
Yankee Stadium
like crazy. The
temperature on
the stadium sign
read 17 degrees.
I didn't know it
could get that
cold! Before
we'd moved to
New Jersey the
year before, I
had lived most
of my life in
warm places
like Florida and
South America.

My stocking cap helped keep my head warm. With my gloves on, and putting my hands inside my coat and under my arms, I was able to keep my hands warm. I couldn't stop shaking, but the shaking helped keep my body a little warmer.

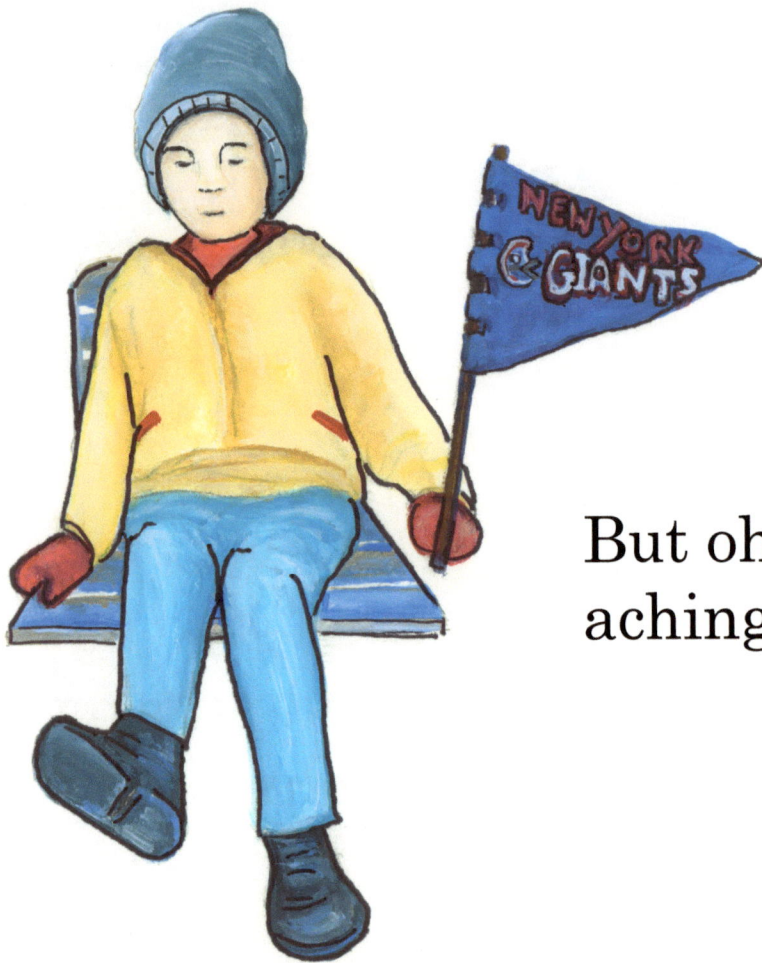

But oh, my
aching toes!

It didn't matter that I
had on two pairs of socks,
tennis shoes, and, on top of
that, my trusty galoshes.

I still couldn't keep my toes warm. Who would have thought ten little tootsies could cause so much pain?

Dad could see that I was hurting.

He came to my rescue.

As the battle went on down on the field between the Giants and the Packers, up in the stands Dad was fighting a battle of his own—keeping my toes warm.

All during the game, I would take my
galoshes and shoes off one foot and put it
in Dad's lap for him to rub the pain out of
my toes. Then, after a while, I switched
feet, and he rubbed the pain out of those
toes. Finally, my toes got to feeling better.
Dad was winning his fight with my cold
feet, and we stayed to watch the whole game.

But how do you rub the pain out of a little boy's heart after he watches his heroes lose the big game, 16-7? I kept asking myself how Del Shofner, Y.A. Tittle, Frank Gifford, Andy Robustelli, Sam Huff and all the rest of my heroes could lose.

I thought my world would never be the same. How could you count on anything in life if you couldn't count on the New York Giants?

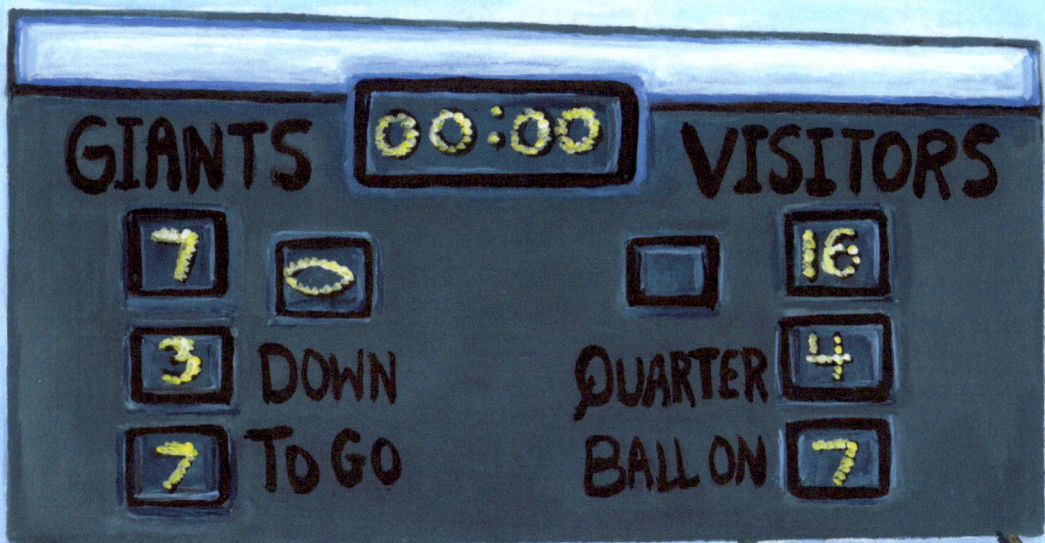

But later, as Dad pulled the car into our garage that cold and dark night, I came to figure out something important about heroes: Sometimes they don't come dressed in shoulder pads, jerseys and helmets. Sometimes they don't score touchdowns. Sometimes they sit in the stands and rub their little boys' toes.

Those are the best heroes of all!

Father and son on the author's wedding day in 1976. "Once again Dad is helping with my cold feet!"

About the Game

As the story reflects, this game has always been special to me for the affection I enjoyed and gained for my dad more than the actual outcome of the game. That has always been my "final score"! At my dad's funeral, 54 years after the game, in 2016, I told this story as a tribute to two of my dad's best qualities: creating possibilities for others to learn and succeed, and being protective of the well-being of others.

As I studied about the 1962 NFL Championship game for this book, I learned many aspects of the game I did not know or remember from my perspective as a nine-year-old. But, many of the events are "frozen" in my memory. The five Giants players I mention in the book were names I remember clearly from all the way back when I was nine. My favorite player was Del Shofner (number 85). After only one year of being a Giants fan, I wanted to grow up and be a wide receiver with a great pair of hands, just like Del Shofner! And I thought his name was cool, too! I well remember the Giants' quarterback, Y.A. Tittle (number 14) and the dashing flanker, Frank Gifford (number 16). I recall Sam Huff (number 70) and Andy Robustelli (number 81) as fierce defensive players who tackled many of the other teams' stars in every game.

When I studied the Giants' 1962 roster, a few other familiar names came fondly to mind: Rosey Brown, Rosey Grier, Jim Katcavage, and Alex Webster.

I did not realize until my research that there were 17 NFL Hall of Famers involved in the game, including the owner of the Giants, Wellington Mara, and Head Coach Vince Lombardi of the Packers. Of the five Giants players I mention in the story, all became Hall of Famers except for my favorite, Del Shofner. Rosey Brown also made the Hall of Fame for the Giants. The Packers had ten Hall of Fame players on the field, including the MVP of the game, middle linebacker Ray Nitschke, quarterback Bart Starr, Jim Taylor, Willie Wood, Willie Davis, Herb Adderley, Paul Hornung, Forrest Gregg, Henry Jordan, and Jim Ringo.

How was I to know, as a new kid in town, how good the Packers were, or that the previous year the Packers had beaten the Giants in the NFL Championship Game played in Green Bay? I now realize more fully that the 1962 Giants and Packers were both historically great teams, and as legendary coach Lombardi said after the game, "I think it was about as fine a football game as I've ever seen." It was a high-quality, physically brutal game in terrible conditions. The New York Giants are still my heroes, but the Packers are no longer my "bad guys."

Lastly, what about the weather? Different accounts say the temperature was 13 degrees or 17 degrees Fahrenheit. This is likely explained by the fact that the winds and temperature definitely worsened during the afternoon. Some accounts say the temperature reached single digits by the time the game ended and that the winds actually increased from the 35-40 mph they were blowing at the start of the game. As bad as the weather was, the Giants fans were tougher. Reports are that only 300 of the roughly 56,000 fans who bought tickets to the game stayed home. The conditions were so cold that a cameraman filming the game got frostbite, and television crews used dugout bonfires to keep their cameras working. A broadcaster, Art Rust, Jr., later described the weather as "barbaric."

Who am I to disagree?

Doug Kauffmann

www.ingramcontent.com/pod-product-compliance
Lightning Source LLC
Chambersburg PA
CBHW041241040426

42445CB00004B/116